Parisian skill
of being Gorgeous

Parisian skill of being Gorgeous

Style lessons from Parisian strangers

Cosy time edition

Parisian skill of being Gorgeous. Style guide. Cosy time edition
ISBN: 9798861309172

Acknowledgements

Thank you to my friend, my student and my teacher Colin Turbett for his help and encouragement.

Thank you to my husband for being ready to spend all his holidays with me in Paris.

Thank you to everyone who showed interest in this book.

Contents

Be attentive, take your time and let those strangers become your friends...

We have all heard about this special skill of French people to dress effortlessly chic despite the occasion, their budget or the weather.

During my last couple of visits to the City of Lights in October 2021, March and December 2022, I captured these beautiful moments simply out of curiosity, but later it gave me the idea for this book.

As many of us know, French people are very mindful of their style and clothing. They shop very consciously to make sure that the pieces they chose will serve them well for decades.

Therefore, I'm daring to say that in this book you will find some classy outfits, which are absolutely timeless. Also, we will try to discover together the French mind-set, their attitude and come up with some simply chic style formulas.

I want to take you with me through some cute little Parisian streets and have a sneak peek at their dynamic life. We will meet total strangers walking, talking, dating, eating, and still being gorgeous.

Be attentive, take your time and let those strangers become your friends...

Part One
Gorgeous while...
dining

Dining, breakfasting, drinking
or smoking, they are always
incredibly chic.

Date your food

Dining, breakfasting, drinking or smoking, they are always incredibly chic.

French people take everything they do very seriously.

A tiny cup of espresso…A quick cigarette… A glass of wine…

It's an art of life, of daily joys, so date them like you would date your desirable second half.

I'm sure you've heard that all Parisians wear black during the winter season... Well, they do gravitate towards much darker colours in winter, but as you will see later, it's not always black. In fact, it's mostly not black.

So… if you are thinking about Classic Parisian and imagining someone in high heels wearing a beret and holding a baguette, then you have never been to Paris!

The truth is This is a Classic Parisian: simple and complicated, put together and falling apart.

If her garments are slightly old-fashioned, she will call them vintage, if she didn't find the right shoes in the lady's section and borrowed her boyfriend's old derbies, she will say, that it's a masculine touch to her outfit; if she didn't have time to brush her hair, she will call it sexy-messy, because the most expensive accessory she is wearing is her attitude.

If you look at her briefly, you think she is wearing all black, but that's not in fact the case.

Does she want to attract your attention? Maybe. Does she care if she doesn't? ...

Her hairband is actually dark grey, and her trousers are dark blue, but all together it

looks like a monochromatic combination of different shades.

Have you spotted these rich dark chocolate waves? Amazing accessorizing itself, isn't it?

Have you spotted these rich dark-chocolate waves?

Take your time!

We popped into this cute corner café called "Leon".
Two girls having their lunch were finishing it with
some tea and cigarettes.

We popped into this cute corner café called "Leon". Two girls having their lunch were finishing it off with some tea and cigarettes. They were having a relaxed conversation, and it was a nice feeling in the air around them.

I couldn't help myself and took a picture. That was my first one. I just wanted to capture this beautiful moment to remind myself that sometimes all we need is to slow down and share our food with someone we love.

Back home, when I started looking at this picture, I noticed the delicate Burberry pattern on one of these girls' sleeves tying together the whole outfit... This lovely, checked print had some beige in it (like her parka and furry vest), some taupe (like her jumper, the trim on her sneakers and this square-shaped medium bag) and navy blue (like her straight-leg jeans and socks).

At that point, I found it quite unusual that she chose darker socks for the light sneakers, but later I discovered, she wasn't the only one using that trick to elongate her legs!

Her friend on the left was wearing a tasteful combination of two very subtle colours: soft breaky-orange and pale blue. Being of the same intensity these two colours complimented each other extremely well.

To finish her outfit, she chose a black structured crossbody bag to tie everything together and off-white sneakers with short tonal socks.

This picture couldn't be more harmonious even if it were staged deliberately. You have a perfect example of how to wear a darker top with a lighter bottom, which makes it look quite fresh and sporty and a classier combination of a darker bottom with a lighter top.

Make an effort despite the weather.

It's raining outside, I'm sitting in the café, finishing an espresso and greeting every woman walking through that door. I want to see this café through their eyes, I want to catch their feelings, I want to understand them better!

My husband sitting beside me is cracking the golden caramel top of his delicious Crème Brulé while I'm trying to crack her style...

And hello our new French lady!

Very simple yet put together. A light beige structured coat, tall burned caramel boots (not new, but well looked after, comfy and elevated), black tights and a black crossbody bag. What makes the whole look more interesting to me is her grey scarf. If it were black or beige, it would look like she was trying too hard, if the scarf had a bright colour, it would make her look more eccentric, and she obviously wants to remain classy.

This lady's coat is quite short and tailored so we cannot see even a sign of a dress or a skirt underneath. I've seen a lot of this type of combination on the streets of Paris: a short, tailored coat (almost looking like a winter dress) paired with tall, fitted boots.

How would you spice up that look Parisian way? Maybe a pair of velvety chocolate pantyhose?

A busy life still has a place for joys

Have you ever considered wearing three different-sized bags all at once and still look elegant? No?

But Voila! This lady just did it!!

Right, let's find out how…

First, she is wearing a beautiful navy coat. It's relaxed yet structured. I suppose this little button at the back allows this coat to change its shape from straight to trapezium in one click.

The whole silhouette is fitted and harmonious. She doesn't have a lot of colours in her outfit, and they all complement each other beautifully.

Flat camel lace-up boots accompanied by the same colour of crossbody bag plus very fitted navy jeans or trousers.

I don't think that the colour of that big sporty bag is a random choice. It's bright and cheery, it's not supposed to be part of the outfit, but strangely enough, it doesn't kill it either.

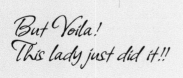

*But Voila!
This lady just did it!!*

*And hair... Natural, curly, wild,
coincidentally matching her bag...*

This is a bag, which is not pretending to be a stylish bag: it's funky, maybe childish, but playful and cool.

And hair… Natural, curly, wild, coincidentally matching her bag and her boots…

*But we don't believe in French-style coincidence.
Do we?*

Make memories...

Now let me take you out for a lovely dinner at "Sarah Bernard", where the waiters don't speak much English, which is always a good sign of an unspoiled authentic café.

Four ladies beside us are having their three-course meal together.

I was absolutely amazed by this cosy and simple colour combination of a tailored grey jacket, a burgundy-wine coloured knitted dress with a matching scarf and caramel leather boots, softening the contrast.

When you read in French books, written by famous Parisian designers and models that coat is a piece to invest in (or at least take very seriously), please believe them!

I can honestly say, I have not seen poorly cuts or thin loose fabrics on French women when it comes to their coats.

I believe they would rather wear a Zara puffer for two winters while saving for a good quality coat, than opt for something bad and cheap which will scream for a replacement next season.

Take a look at this perfectly structured grey coat... It's almost standing by itself. Is it not a good test when buying your next one?

Make memories...

Perfectly fitted, or slightly loose, made of at least 70 per cent virgin wool, preferably lined (even better if with a natural fabric), suits your complexion and will serve you for years.

This kind of coat can be your saviour on all occasions especially on that early Sunday morning when you agreed to have breakfast out with your friends but feel exactly like those scrambled eggs which have been just served to the next table.

On that note, let's leave our Parisians to dine in peace and have a sneak peek at those ones, who are browsing through the shops hoping to find a perfect garment or popping to the weekly market to source some ingredients for a delicious meal later.

Parisian skill of being Gorgeous

Gorgeous while... shopping

Gorgeous while...
shopping

Tell your own story

Even though this lady is wearing a luxurious designer bag and pleated satin trousers, her look reminds me of a gorgeous sunny day in Savanna…

It is beautifully executed chic and elegant style with a twist of a safari allusion.

I can picture her having a double espresso from a little white porcelain cup on the terrace this morning or gracefully feeding gigantic elephants with some freshly cut bananas this afternoon.

Maybe it's just this abundance of khaki that speaks to me that way, or the shape of her slick (and no doubt designer) hat... I don't know exactly, but something about her style is more than just beautiful pieces thrown together. It's an attitude to express and a story to tell...

If you have a closer look, you will notice, that all her items have two interesting and very controversial characteristics: they all have a structured shape and relaxed style.

Her long coat is simple and straight but doesn't have any complicated details or a belt to tighten around the waist.

Her trousers are very fluid, but have lots of vertical pleats, which allows them to be soft and structured at the same time. Her hat is very round shaped, but this shape is solid!

Her trainers have some contrasting yet delicate curvy lines.

Even her structured quilted bag is so relaxed that it prefers to stay opened.

Take it easy

Saturday mornings…

Take it easy

Lots of little squares in the middle of Paris filling up with market stalls, offering multiple choices of fresh fruits and vegetables, different kinds of meat and exotic delicacies.

Lots of ladies (and gentlemen) take their big foldable bags, shopping trolleys and even wicker baskets down to the market to fill them with seasonal food and Sunday treats.

That was my gem, spotted on a December Saturday morning in one of those little markets. This lady had a nice, neat bob (not really styled any particular way), and she was wearing a classic grey coat paired with sporty grey (still wide) trousers and funky pink trainers.

If you draw an invisible line in the middle of her body, and look at the top and the bottom separately, you most likely would think that they belong to two different (age, style and mind-set) people. And yet it's one lady: comfortable, unpredictable and still chic.

This lady has enough taste and experience to pull a classy look together, but she also wants to be comfortable, so she is happy to trade her suede ankle boots for something a little bit sportier and spicier. Love it! Do you?

Make friends with your clothes

Have you ever come across those articles pointing at the most popular jeans among French women? Like those perfect vintage Levi's you need to hunt for all your life? In this perfect vintage denim mid-wash colour with a straight leg and a very curvy bum…. Here is my opinion… Look through the 60+ images of the real Parisians in this book and tell me if you've seen even a single one wearing them!

Do you know what kind of jeans a French woman prefers? Those ones, she already owns. They can be long and flared with pockets, so she can fit some leggings underneath, as Paris can be pretty chilly in December, or they could be wide and cropped as she wants to emphasise her snake patterned ankle boots, or they could be skinny as she has very toned legs to show. There is no such thing as a perfect pair of jeans, but there is "a perfect pair for you".

Now, we are talking… Very statement long flared jeans (like I just described earlier) paired with a funky volume jacket for a balanced look. Something tells me that a lot of French people have their "thought through" outfit combinations and their "capsule wardrobe" but it is slightly different from what we think about it.

French "capsule" is based on finding a perfect match for every single item in your wardrobe, but it doesn't mean that all your items are supposed to mix and match, because that would mean they all need to be neutral, basic and universal, which makes them less unique and very common (and that's what French people definitely don't want).

I believe that "Je ne sais quoi" comes not just from finding your perfect items but more from making those unique and unexpected combinations.

Make friends with your clothes.

Be curious!

This is a great classic example (or two, which is even better) of a smart casual weekend style. You can see it in Parisians who browse through the little local markets, cafes and shop displays hunting for a new treasure.

Have you noticed that most colours we've seen on outerwear are not as simple as they might seem from the first look? If blue, then with a hint of lavender, if yellow, then with a spoonful of mustard in it. Understated and clean but never too blunt.

The lady on the left is wearing a casual and cosy yellow corduroy jacket with dark grey faded skinny jeans (and according to Parisians, it's still very much "ok" to wear them), light grey socks and white leather sneakers.

And I would like to take a minute here to make a point, that French people obviously have been told something different on the subject of socks styling!

So, rather than trying to match your socks with the colour of your shoes, try to match them with your trousers or alternatively opt for a transitional colour! Genius! It makes the whole look harmonious, doesn't break your leg and doesn't make your footwear look separated from the rest of the outfit!

Now let's move to the lady on the right...

An absolutely beautiful long structured violet-blue coat, balanced by straight full-length denim and dark sneakers with yellow stripes for the additional sporty, boyish vibe.

By the way, I didn't see a lot of dressing gown type of coats so popular everywhere else at the moment.

That's a perfect example of masculine and feminine happily living one next to another! They don't compete because they are very much colour coordinated and they don't argue as one of them is proportionally so much bigger than another.

And please don't forget to add to the feminine side of her look this gorgeous red wavy hair! But she doesn't want to appear too romantic or classy, she would like to tell us about her strong character and complicated personality –
that's where her jeans and sneakers come into play.

That's a perfect example of masculine-feminine happily living one next to another! They don't compete because they are very much colour coordinated.

Gorgeous while...

on the go

03

02

01

Belle maman!

French women are famous for highlighting their strong sides and disguising weaker ones.

As we all can imagine, after having a baby, it could take a while before mum gets back to her usual shape and size (especially in the area around her tummy).

Some new mums feel uncomfortable with their new self and try to wear loose baggy clothes all over their body, but what if your legs are still in very good shape (and I believe they are from pushing this pram everywhere)? Why not show them? Why not make them give everyone the impression of your shape and size? The human eye unconsciously assumes that the rest of the body is fit and toned as well!

What a gorgeous game of proportions and colours! A loose black cape (which is already chic itself) paired with thick black tights or leggings and spiced up with equal intensity but contrasting colour accessories like a hat with gloves in red and trainer-style boots in ocean green.

Does she look like she's given up on herself? No. Does she look like she is trying too hard to prove that she is still in the game? Absolutely not!

She is comfortable, confident, and chic.

Belle maman!

Another example of a cool mum is this lovely lady in an earthy-coloured outfit. She has a classic dark green coat, paired with straight cropped navy jeans (you will see a lot of them in the next few chapters), lighter green flat ankle boots and navy socks.

It's quite an interesting trick I've seen in Paris a lot when cropped trousers are paired with socks of the same colour.

Visually it gives the impression of thin ankles without shortening the length of the leg and adds a little bit of a cheeky attitude to the outfit. I think it's absolute genius.

As we can tell from the strap, she has a brown bag and a brown scarf. She doesn't wear anything extremely trendy or colourful, but this colour combination definitely gives her outfit this effortless, put-together feeling we all are aiming for.

Cool maman

Only in France have I seen so many
people wearing unusual shapes or colours
and looking radiant in them.

Know your colours!

Oh, I remember that one! You should have seen me running through the streets of Paris chasing this gorgeous Parisienne, so I could take a closer look!

She had a beautiful velour chocolate coat, voluminous caramel hair, navy trousers and flat brown boots. Those colours were extremely flattering to her complexion and her clothes looked like an extension of her features.

That's where you can find this crucial difference between French girls and the rest of the world: while we spend lots of time trying to catch up on the latest trends and standards, they are mastering their skill of understanding themselves, knowing their complexion, proportion, shape and strengths.

Only in France have I seen so many people wearing unusual shapes or colours and looking radiant in them.

And there's quite a simple explanation for that:
it's not the colours they know so well, it's themselves!

Find your silhouette!

You know what the most obvious sign is that you've spotted a true Parisienne? Look at the rhythm this lady walks with. If she is taking a peaceful stroll, you are looking in the wrong direction. You need someone who is rushing through the streets of Paris like she is on a mission!

Here we can see a classic combination of a Navy coat, straight black jeans and a pair of beige ankle boots. On top of that a cheerful multi-coloured tote bag and a graphic strap of unseen handbag. We can't say that her look is extremely colourful or layered, but it's very Parisian…

A similar colour choice for the coat and jeans elongates the silhouette, while beige footwear adds some lightness to the outfit and elevates the whole look. I would say that the motto of this outfit is: "Let's not overcomplicate our clothes, life is complicated enough!"

Just a quick note on the theme of choosing your canvas (or fabric) tote bag: opt for something including colours you wear in your outfits the most. It doesn't need to be boring and maybe it doesn't need to be one colour either, as you probably don't want to add to your outfit another solid colour block of navy or black or red.

A similar colour choice for the coat and jeans elongates the silhouette, while beige footwear adds some lightness to the outfit and elevates the whole look.

Embrace your lifestyle!

"Parisian scarves" is another mysterious subject we can talk about forever. They are never picked randomly even if it looks like that. There is a lot of thought put into that "random looking bright scarf effortlessly thrown over the shoulder".

The Parisienne with her daily routine and hundreds of places to be during the day is still very faithful to her style. She is practical yet chic.

A classic brown tailored checked coat, supported by the dark burgundy handbag, paired with blue jeans and a very similar toned checked blue scarf; a pair of dark navy suede boots with medium pointy heels and straight-leg jeans tucked into them.

What kind of thoughts run through your head when you look at this lady?

I think she knows herself pretty well, she accepts her lifestyle and adds as much chic and sophistication to her daily looks as she possibly can.

She has a wide
selection of
well-trusted
items, which were
introduced to
her wardrobe at
different periods
of time, and they
all complement
each other.

Also, she
probably has
a handful of
scarves which
happily help her
to marry different
parts of her outfit
together.
I believe she
likes to wear this
checked navy one
on days when
she has her blue
denim paired with
something more
subtle and plain.

Cultivate your chic!

Parisian by birth… Elegant, chic, stylish and even slightly eccentric.

Nothing screams, but the message is very clear… Subtle colours, structured shapes and that desirable "Je ne sais quoi"…

Grey cape coat paired with straight brown velvet trousers and black ankle boots, a structured hat and a semi-structured medium-size bag.

When we met this lady on a Parisian street, I had to ask myself where she was going. She definitely didn't look like she had made an extra effort to look good. It was rather an old habit of looking chic, put together and true to her style. But the size of her bag told me that she was not out for a coffee with an old friend (in which case she would have had a small Chanel wallet with her), she wasn't going for her grocery shopping either (because as we know, most Parisiens use their trolley or a foldable tote for that occasion).

Where was she going? I couldn't stop thinking about her beautiful, elegant look, her light scent of a classy perfume, when she passed us and I imagined her gorgeous apartment in one of the old Haussmann's buildings with the spacious high ceiling, authentic paintings on the walls and dark-green heavy velvet curtains.

She was the quintessence of Classic Paris.

She was a perfect stranger.

There is a fine line between "simple and "plain". Plain could be boring, but simple is always chic.

Parisians don't do "plain". Their simple outfits are well-orchestrated and beautifully colour-coordinated. Nobody wants to appear boring, but some still prefer to stay discreet, understated and quiet.

Find your comfort zone!

For example, this lady... She is wearing a long dark navy coat, straight light blue, slightly turned-up jeans and (attention!) this where it gets more complicated: dark navy socks and multi-coloured red trainers.

Classy and feminine top paired with masculine playful bottom.

These little details add an attitude, youth, a little bit of eccentricity and (I bet this wasn't the main reason) warmth.

Her long dark coat looks so balanced not only because of the bright trainers and rolled jeans, but also because of that lovely wavy chestnut hair and a beigy-grey shopping bag warming up the dark colour palette of her outfit.

Sport doesn't argue with the style!

And voila! Another high-speed lady! Sporty yet chic. When do they learn to do it? At primary school? How could it look so good while feeling so seamless?

I believe it's a well-trusted combination of accessories in the same colour palette with a neutral base. All colours are fairly cool and refreshing, so that's why the whole look appears zesty and vital.

The main role here (in my opinion) plays this perfect proportion of the straight puffy jacket, which falls right to the mid-hip level and slightly flared (rather than slim or straight) full-length jeans. It elongates the silhouette, lightens the lower part of the body and adds some feminine vibe from the 70s.

She looks very cosy and comfortable. I can see her nipping out to the grocery store, sitting on the bench reading a book or pushing a pram. She doesn't need to worry about her clothes too much (as it's mostly a dark colour palette) or about a change in the weather (as I bet her jacket is water and wind-resistant).

Saying all that, she still doesn't look like she was dressing in the dark or threw on everything her eye caught first.

But let's not give up, this skill is achievable! We still have so many more pages to go through and so many looks to crack!

Sport doesn't argue with the style!

Stick to your basics!

Did I tell you that navy is the new black? So I did! But did I tell you that it's not a faux pas anymore to combine one with another? Yes, as you can see, lots of people on the streets of Paris prefer navy blue coats and jackets to black ones, but it doesn't mean they are going to betray their good, safe and classy choice of footwear in noir as well.

So, how to marry two similar dark, but still competing colours if you want to wear your navy coat with black shoes/boots? Well, I've seen two options: first is to add some faded black/grey in between (like those leggings in the picture) or simply pair your navy coat with jeans in any shade of blue. It always does the trick.

Another interesting detail about this look is that the coat, which is actually a trench coat (and this happens a lot in Paris) is made of a good quality, thick and durable material, which makes it a perfect companion not only through the autumn, but during the winter season as well.

A statement tote in black balances the same colour in the lower part of the body (loafers) and white writing on it adds a contemporary feel.

The secret is that instead of wearing a massive furry jacket (which some Parisians also do) they have simply mastered the art of layering to be able to stay faithful to their style even in much colder weather and retain their chic and effortless look.

Appreciate the seasons!

Winter... Cold... Dark...Wet...

Some of us opt for the brighter colours to boost our energy level, others head off to warmer countries for a bit of sunshine, but not Parisians...

They stay with their beloved beige and grey city, faithfully waiting for the time of floral dresses, strappy sandals and wicker straw bags. Meanwhile, they will drink more coffee and wine, pull out of their wardrobes their thickest scarves and remain chic and slightly grumpy.

We all know that French people prefer seasonal veg over imported ones, seasonal meals over exotic recipes.

Why go out of your way when it comes to dressing?

A beautiful example of a young woman in black heeled boots and a belted navy coat. Very seasonally appropriate, put together and understated at the same time. The fine cotton tote adds a little romantic note to the look by using a slightly out-of-season fabric and this compliments her long warm scarf, wrapped around the neck.

Most Parisians look like they have just come out of a black-and-white movie.

You cannot see a lot of colours on them, but your eye is still able to define some shades and patterns.

Others look like someone took a bright blue (or red or green) pen and splashed a little bit of colour to the picture, which was originally supposed to be monochromatic as well.

Parisian skill of being Gorgeous

Gorgeous while...

on wheels

You make the rules

Shall we run a small test to see how Parisian you are?

Ready?

Let's say that I've invited you to have a little ride on the bikes to the grocery store four arrondissements away. We might pop into a cafe for a quick cappuccino afterwards.

What would you wear?

If your answer doesn't involve heels, I'm afraid you have some work to do! Would you like me to explain why? We all know that Parisian women love to be practical and comfortable but remain feminine at any cost.

If you ride a bike in the city, you will probably tie your hair back in some sort of a loose ponytail or bun. You don't want it to smell like a city when you come home.

Technically you could wear a skirt but should opt for a pair of jeans or trousers to give yourself as much freedom as your journey might require.

You wouldn't wear a beautiful flowy jacket either as it might get jammed between the wheels.

So, what are your options for showing your feminine side? That's right! Your ankles and your heels!!!

You don't need to go crazy and wear that kind of heels you even struggle to walk in for a bike ride, but consider a pair of cute block-heeled boots, firmly attached to your feet so you don't need to worry that they might slip off on the busy junction.

Let this lady be an inspiration for you and give you a little kick-start!

Let this lady be an inspiration for you and give you a little kick-start!

Keep it simple.

And Voila! Another chic French lady is getting ready to ride a bike.

How to remain classy and effortless while wearing heels and even a short skirt (o-la-la!)?

First, try to mute your colour palette. Let's leave our floral skirts and linen dresses till the summertime.

Second, go for warm, thick and structured fabrics. These will not only keep you cosy during your city ride but also look very season-appropriate.

Add to your monochrome outfit a couple of cheerful accents to avoid the look of a grumpy old librarian.

And don't forget your gloves, your smile and your cigarettes! I'm not advertising this naughty habit to anyone, but a sophisticated ritual of a slow cigarette and a little espresso is still very popular in France.

I don't smoke, but I have a pack of my own, which I bought in Paris a couple of years ago. Sometimes I take them with me on long journeys to add this extra feeling of freedom to my trip.

If you decide to get your own "freedom token" make sure to check with your airline where exactly you are allowed to carry it so as not to stand the later embarrassment of opening your suitcase in front of all passengers on your flight, fishing for this cigarette pack in your bottomless suitcase, because apparently, you should take them in your hand luggage. Seems like a lot of trouble for someone who doesn't even smoke. But that's my guilty pleasure.

Go bold!

How aesthetically pleasing Paris is! Its buildings look so classy and sophisticated, providing the perfect blank canvas for any shoot, whether it's a professionally staged movie scene or a quick "moment capture" for a curious soul like me.

Those buildings, carefully curated by the best architects and designers can teach you about Parisian style more than any book would! This gorgeous and simple combination of beige facades with light-grey mansards and an occasional pop of colour (that's when the eye catches these bright-red or green roofs of a corner café).

Let's have a look at this lady on the bike. I need to admit that she is not wearing heels, but first, she is in a minority and second, she had a good reason.

Do you remember we were discussing that French women like to keep it simple? She is already wearing a beautiful, very feminine colour lilac coat. If she paired it with heels or a skirt she could appear overdressed and that's obviously not her goal. She wants to keep it cool and understated.

Let's have a look at this lady on the bike.

Be a rebel!

So, "style" or "comfort"?

I believe if you were born and raised as a true Parisian that wouldn't be a hard question to answer. Your style is your comfort. It's your sanctuary, it's your safe zone. It cuts a long story short explaining to people who you are before you have even said a word. You have found your "Je ne sais qoui", you are not willing to compromise and now you just need to figure out how to incorporate your unique self-expression into every season and occasion.

Sometimes you just go bold and wear your favourite open-heel leather clogs in December while riding a bike (like this lady on the right). She had a pair of soft cosy socks, matching the colour of her shoes and navy tights, making the whole outfit so feminine and authentic at the same time. Look at her posture, her confidence!

And now look at the woman on the left... She is so funky, cool and faithful... Faithful to her own style! Her bold patterns, her colour combination, her strong and dramatic look. She is another true Parisian. A free spirit in a beautiful vase. It looks like she discovered that she is unique a long time ago and now is just playing with it, twisting and spinning her loud statement pieces while keeping them tamed by the old, trusted classics (dark polo-neck and dark blazer).

I was wondering who could be considered more rebellious: the lady, who dares to wear her bright checked trousers in the city of sophisticated black and navy tones or the other one, who refuses to change her summer shoes just because it's coming to Christmas time?

Daring is sexy!

Do you still think that mini-skirt paired with high heels is the sexiest combination??? What about a Harley and heels???

Just look at her! All in dark, slim-fit clothes, leather jacket and gloves. She looks so delicate and feminine beside her big steel horse.

We don't need to go as far as to pair our feminine look with something masculine, but I definitely know that this combination works! Do you know why I think so?

My husband, who is usually more interested in historical buildings and ice cream parlours than in discussing people's outfits, pointed at her while we were crossing the road and said: "Look! She is so tiny on that big bike! And she is wearing high heels! Is she that Parisienne you are after?"

Daring is sexy!

Part two
Style rules no one talks about

A statement coat for an understated look

I believe that every Parisienne has her statement coat in the perfect size, shape and attitude, reflecting her personality the most. If you think about it, it makes perfect sense: it's the largest piece of the fabric you wear throughout the whole year. It covers from 50 to 90 per cent of your body, so it better be chic, good quality and tell people a lot about you, before you even dive into a conversation about contemporary philosophy or a new patisserie just round the corner.

We hear a lot, that to impress people with your social status you need to have a luxurious bag, fancy shoes and designer sunglasses. The rest can be from any high street shop. That's where the road splits. Following this idea lots of people buy unaffordable accessories to impress others, while the French know **the only person, they really want to impress is themselves**. They want to be emotionally comfortable in what they are wearing and it needs to be true to their own brand, to their personal style. Starting from an early age, they are carefully curating their staple, reliable, basic wardrobe.

This is a perfect example of a timeless, classy yet modern coat in a gorgeous deep burgundy colour, paired with flat camel Chelsea boots and burgundy-toned tights to make an easy and smooth colour transition from the top to the bottom. Do any of these elements seem like a random choice? I don't think so... Does it look too matchy-matchy? Absolutely not!

> 66
>
> *So, maybe all this time when we were trying to solve a mystery of Parisian charm, we were looking in the wrong direction? Maybe it's not only Breton and Red lips? Maybe it's a very fine skill of pairing different parts of the outfit together, combining shapes and shades? Maybe that's a real secret of the French stye? Have a think about it...*

Maybe that's a real secret of a French stye?

Find your BFF!

Long and distant, short and cheeky, medium and soft. Your coat is like your Best Friend! You've been through a lot together (with some coats you can tell that), He knows all your Exes, you know exactly where the hole is in His pocket. You are almost inseparable. You are ready to cheat on Him only with His Best Friend your Beige Trench coat. And I believe that the French version of a famous phrase sounds like **"Show me your coat and I can tell who you are"**.

This chapter turns out to be more philosophical, but we all can agree, that since we stopped wearing clothing just for the "covering body" purposes, the most important message we send to the world is by dressing a certain way and we are all trying to work out how to deliver the right one!

That was a very "attitudinal" coat, spotted on a very young, very "attitudinal" woman. With some of them it seems like their coat is almost an extension of their personality.

The young, cool and confident lady in this picture is wearing a long grey double-breasted coat reminding one of a classic trench coat made with a soft and structured wool fabric.

Black high-top Converse, supported by the grey long-sleeve hand warmers, separated from a sweater (I've seen it from the front). This little detail adds not only an extra cosy feel to the look but makes it more colour-coordinated while remaining effortless.

66

I've noticed that a lot of Parisian ladies have their unique style items, which makes generalization pretty impossible! For some of them it's a shape of the trousers, showing their delicate ankles, for some bright gloves to spice up their monochromatic outfit, for some a very long knitted scarf, perfectly balancing a small collar of the coat.

The only formula working for them all is "Listen to yourself, what you want to tell is unique. Just say it!".

Embrace the power of colour!

Are French women afraid of the natural process of ageing?

Absolutely not!

Why would they?

Now, slowly gravitating from their greys and beiges to more rich and eccentric colours, they feel like their style can take one step forward. They already know their safe combinations and trusted items. Why not to add a little crazy detail (or two) instead of appearing like an old boring lady?

An eccentric blue coat paired with dark grey fitted slim jeans and flat black ankle boots, a multicoloured dusty green scarf and a dark green headband. We don't see from this angle if our lady has a small shoulder bag (my memory doesn't recall it either), but what we can see is this bright grassy-green fishnet bag, holding her groceries.

She does look very enthusiastic, and I think that's a trick with bright colours: despite wanting it or not, they lift your mood, your spirit and even your attitude. But the French stay French by muting everything else in the look. They definitely do not see themselves as a potential battlefield for the competing bright colours.

Make it safe but play it cool!

That's my personal favourite! Long and warm, straight and structured, vibrant and practical.

You simply can't go wrong with a basic, good quality mid to maxi length coat, made from good durable fabric, lined or not.

Navy blue is a new approach on trusted black. Still classy but slightly more casual.

What makes this coat a statement? Well… Its length, its uncompromising structured shape, its quality.

This minimalistic coat paired with nice low-heeled ankle boots in shiny leather and slim grey jeans to define narrow ankles and lighten the silhouette.

The safe colour combination of a navy coat with a light sage crossbody bag, supported by the same colour scarf in a slightly more intense shade.

On top of that the whole look spiced up by the red canvas tote.

You know, what I've noticed? These totes... They almost live a life of their own... They appear in the most unexpected places in absolutely random colour combinations, adding to the look a spontaneous, complicated and even mysterious touch...

They make you wonder: "Did she buy this tote bag? Well... What an interesting choice of colour... Did she get it as a complimentary gift, while shopping for some clothes, shoes or books? What story does it tell???"

Make it safe but play it cool!

For the love
of colour

La vie est rouge...

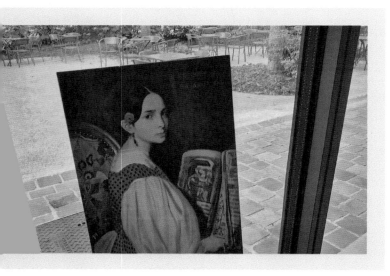

As we all know, French people like to add colourful accessories to their outfits. I would say that amongst the most popular colours for the bags, shoes and scarves would be camel (of all shades from beige to chocolate), green (mostly cool-toned and very refreshing) and red (from orange to raspberry).

Considering the most popular colour for outerwear is navy (or black) it makes perfect sense to add a little bit of a vibrant colour to the plain and timeless outfit.

On this lady we can see a long black coat paired with black tights and three iconic accents in red, wisely spread across the look: a red and black scarf, a red bag and red lace-up shoes.

Why doesn't the whole outfit look too polished? I believe, that's because it has a slight degree of intensity and warmth between the colours of all three pieces.

Harmonious, but not matching in style.

Grey is a gentle black…

Style doesn't have an age, a gender or even a sense of cold…
One thing is to see a young girl, surrounded by her friends, wearing a bare minimum of clothing in the middle of winter, rushing to the party in her sparkly sandals, trying not to shiver too much, making everyone feel sad and sorry for her. It's a completely different story, when you have a well and warmly dressed lady, embracing the winter season in her own way by showing her delicate, slim ankles and keeping the rest of her body toasty.

It's more like a sign of respect for the city she has been dating for the last 50 years and it's a sign of her style and a reflection of her passionate personality. Her passion for life, for her little daily rituals, for herself.

Dressing for someone else is a dead-end road and it leads nowhere. What if your effort is not acknowledged? Will it not defeat the purpose straight away and ruin your enthusiasm?

But what if the person you are doing this for is yourself? It's the only person, who has always been by your side, who has seen the best and the worst of you. Why not make an extra effort for this closest person in the world? Just try! It's worth it!

I believe, that the feeling of "put together" comes from knowing yourself, accepting yourself and trying your best just for yourself. This sense of self-belief, this radiance, this harmony comes from within.

I believe this lady just popped out to the grocery store in her neighbourhood. She loves her colours, and she knows them well. This delicate combination of a long and soft toffee coat with light grey (almost silver) accessories makes the whole look very elegant, very classy but also relaxed. Just look at her slender ankles in these light grey tights to match her beautiful suede court shoes.

❝
Please don't try this trick if you are visiting Paris in December as you might end up spending the rest of your holiday in bed with a terrible cold! You need to be born near Senna to brave this winter style and I bet she has been practising her aristocratic winter approach since the 70-s.

Chocolate is good for your style
and your mood!

I spotted her on the way to the Louvre's courtyard and imagined straight away that she could be a curator of one of their classic exhibitions… Then I pictured her as a young lecturer at uni, who just wanted to pop in and double-check something for one of her classes.

But the next thing that crossed my mind was that she just prefers these melancholic and intellectual colours of her outfit for none of those reasons and passes through the courtyard to go for some lunch. With her book. I insist that a book must be involved.

And I would like to add, that it's not a simple sweet milk chocolate. It's a perfect rich dark chocolate truffle from one of those famous Parisian chocolatiers you can buy only in France...

So, what does our Parisienne prefer? Total look or tonal look? What do we have in here? A pair of tall chocolate boots with a pinch of red undertone in them, a toffee parka jacket, a dark brown bag and brown hair.

It's definitely a tonal look (as those colours don't have an exact match) but what makes it tasteful and graceful? Well... She adds some layers and volume to the look by allowing her items to be slightly different.

Still medium dark, still neutral, but with different undertones in them. That is what makes the look so comfortable for the eye to see and so complicated for the mind to read. It's a fovourite French game: catch my style if you can... Can you not? Well, just admire it then!

For the love of Chocolate!!!

Caramel is too soft to deny!

It was a really chilly day, and everyone pulled their cosiest clothes out of the wardrobe. I've seen lots of long coats, massive scarves and red noses.

Even the bravest were not sitting outside the café anymore. We all sadly admitted that winter had arrived. It was even more interesting to hunt for some unusual style combinations that day.

And that was one of them. I need to say, that it's not a classic Parisian look, but it attracted my attention.

Have I seen a lot of UGGS on the streets of Paris? Definitely not. But when I did, the outfits were very much unexpected, and this lady is a great example!

It's a very unusual but still working combination of extremely casual (I would say even minimal effort) footwear and a luxuriously smooth, classy caramel coat. I'm pretty sure it would not work so well if those two pieces were completely different colours as they are already from two different worlds, but it's all about the shades, the tones and combinations…

Her medium size semi-structured bag is a perfect colour match for her boots, and this sporty soft hat in a light beige colour just proves that the footwear choice wasn't random. It's a thought-through **ironic combination of high and low**. And that's the reason why it looks so polished.

Beige is always fresh!

Remember, I told you that Parisians wear their trench coats all year round? I wasn't lying.

If they happen to find something working for them once, they hold on to it pretty tight. While the rest of the world reaches out for a warmer jacket and immediately faces the question "Right, what am I going to wear it with now?" as soon as the temperature drops, the French just add an extra layer underneath and keep rocking their favourite autumn outfit.

Just a quick note about the total looks. As I mentioned earlier, I've noticed that French people much prefer the challenge of styling different but not obviously matching pieces in one look rather than having an endless wardrobe with perfect matches.

However, some of them are very comfortable wearing beige as a total look. Not so much younger people: in their case, it only would be the total navy or black with a pair of bright sneakers. Slightly older ladies though, if going for the total look, will opt for much lighter colours like beige, cream and caramel.

The same day, different spot. Sun came out and Paris immediately cheered up.

Slightly chunkier block-heeled boots with light cream soles (another very popular detail in France) and a knitted cream scarf add to the classy trench and hat a little bit of dynamic, texture and joy.

Classic medium, probably vintage bag (simply judging by the style and shape of it), resembles different details of the outfit and pulls it all together.

Simply by changing your bag and hat for a brighter and sportier one, you can transform the overall style and lose a couple of years as well.

Prints and patterns

Style and passion

Find a match!

I have probably seen more prints on Parisian streets than I managed to capture, but here is the thing: they are never picked randomly!

Prints and patterns are built into the existing wardrobe.

How do I know that?

Well, unless she bought this scarf, this bag and these trousers all in one day (which I doubt), then she put a lot of consideration into building her outfit to make sure that those spicy new trousers would fit well with her existing colour palette.

I believe this way of incorporating new prints into your wardrobe is absolutely genius!

She has picked the softest colour in the print of the trousers (which is dark purple) and added different shades of it to her outfit: a light purple scarf and a deep plum crossbody bag.

The lesson here is: pick your accent colours and stick to them. Don't buy lots of different colourful items hoping they will work together. They will not, unless you make them! And how to do that?

Is it only me or does it seem like the side of her paper bag matches her trousers as well?

To start with pick one print and forget about the rest just now.

Make sure that this print contains some colours of your existing loved wardrobe.

Keep the rest plain and make it a statement!

Reveal yourself!

We had just finished our traditional French breakfast at the little corner cafe across the road and were ready for the new adventures of the day. Suddenly I just stopped. I see her…

My new perfect stranger.

How much can you tell from the first look at someone? How many pages of their book you can read straight away?

Most likely, just a cover. That's why it's so important to keep your inner and outer world in balance and when your cover doesn't reflect the book's content anymore, it's time to change.

Do yourself a favour and don't confuse people who are interested in your book with a deceiving cover.

She was hesitant, feminine, mysterious… Her delicate dainty floral dress (yes, I can't prove it, but I'm pretty sure it's a dress) was combined with a roomy dark blue (almost black) coat, sporty-looking boots and a blue crossbody bag.

That's an interesting combination of sport, romantic and casual!

The jacket and the dress are close enough colour-wise not to break the silhouette in the middle at hip level and the skirt (or dress) has this gorgeous almost summertime fluidity, which helps the whole outfit appear much softer.

Quite often we can see that full navy looks can be spiced up by red, caramel or white accessories, but if a crossbody bag is chosen in one of those colours instead of blue the charming simplicity of that look is ruined.

Get classic support!

Halfway through the book and we still haven't talked about checked print?

Are you sure we are discussing French style here???

Well... Let's correct this unforgivable mistake.

If we were looking at spring or summertime staple pieces in the Parisian wardrobe, we would definitely be talking about this famous checked (preferably vintage) blazer you can see on every corner of the city. Happy to introduce his big brother – the checked coat! Not as popular amongst young people as the blazer, but it definitely takes its well-earned place in French wardrobes.

Length and style-wise it's always classy, tailored, short to midi, paired with less structured items for this perfectly balanced but not too formal look.

On this lady, as we can see, it's paired with full-length flared jeans, a warm cosy scarf in cream (not white!) colour, matching one of the colours of the coat and a black (possibly navy) knitted hat.

The overall look is very simple and understated with a little classy and chic twist.

That's exactly how we like it!

●

Lengths and shapes

The vibrant and playful orange colour elevates the look, sets the tone and keeps her cool.

Be cosy & stay cool!

Do you think French people know a special secret? Kind of unwritten rules of being effortlessly gorgeous despite the fact of what they are wearing...

Let's not get overwhelmed by making it sound impossible! Shall we try to break the look and hopefully crack her style?

I need to admit, that her companion is dressed very cosily and harmoniously too, but it's fairly easy to break down: the whole look in creams and browns with a mustard jacket in-between to make this perfect French connection. All fabrics are matte, and all pieces are square-shaped. Perfect cappuccino! Voila!

This lady on the other hand is a perfect player: she has a gorgeous velvety-grey furry coat, covering about 80 per cent of her body but she adds some incredibly spicy details to it not to appear old-fashioned or classy.

So, what's the best way to shake the good winter classics? Well, obviously by adding a summer bucket hat! Of course, it's not a real summer hat, it's a much warmer version of it in a slightly shiny nylon fabric with the contrasting sporty detail, matching her bag strap and possibly trainers.

The vibrant and playful orange colour elevates the look, sets the tone and keeps her cool.

Not to lean too much towards the sporty side, this lady adds a pair of fluid black trousers instead of jeans to smarten up the look and confuse us even more! Voila!

Look inside!

Every time you see a well-dressed person (and I don't mean expensively dressed, I mean just "put together") you can almost sense this extra confidence coming from them knowing themselves.

Style is not just about the style after all, it's all about well-being, about saying what you want to say, doing what you want to do and feeling good about it.

If you are lucky to be born into a family, where you can see great examples of people connected to their true style, to their passion, to their body, then you have an advantage, but if you (like myself and lots of others) grew up in surroundings that were a little far from style-thinking, please join the club of lost souls who are looking for answers...

And if you continue to be curious and attentive, I promise, that soon you will find your path, you will find your voice, you will reconnect with yourself.

As you can see, this lucky lady on the right has quite interestingly dressed parents. A classier dad with his brown corduroy trousers paired with a straight black jacket and a more eccentric mum, who is not afraid of showing her flamboyant side.

This funky coat is supported by a short haircut and cropped wide trousers. While being muted, her look appears very colour-coordinated. Her structured coat has two block colours and the darker part of it not only matches the trousers, but elongates the lower part of her body, defeating the idea that "cropped and wide pants always shorten your legs". It's a very strong, quite a rebellious look.

No wonder their daughter is not afraid of her bright and colourful self-expression! Green coat with a shawl collar, turned-on blue jeans,

an orange bag and white and orange sneakers. It is a message there. It must be. It's a young, vibrant and adventurous person, who likes to stay cosy while drawing in her own style colouring book with her favourite pencils.

Experiment!

There are fewer ways to unleash your femininity in the winter…
And showing your delicate slim ankles is one of the tools most
French women seem to be using!

#1

#2

#3

Right, what do we have … A soft cropped square jacket in this beautiful caramel colour, paired with black culottes and black ankle boots, showing some leg space in between. As always, with a closer look, we can see not an obvious match between the sole of these patent block-heeled boots and the colour of her jacket.

Every single item of her outfit falls somewhere between casual and classy: the style, proportions, choice of colours…Everything apart from the length of her trousers and her bright checked (still colour coordinated) foldable tote bag.

This style combination is clearly helping us to read a message: it's a modern classy French lady who accepts her feminine side as well as the boyish part of her personality. She likes her basics and classics but doesn't mind experimenting from time to time!

The power of accessories

Tame your beast!

Believe it or not, but I've seen a lot of leopard print on the streets of Paris. Not in the shape of a coat or jumper, but small, sexy and spicy details, like a total black look with some leopard ballet flats, a small leopard bag or even a bag strap detail. If added in moderation, these prints can bring to your look this desirable effortless, **"sexy and free"** feeling. And that's how the French do it.

****

As you can see from the picture, the best companion for this long navy coat is the red façade of the café, but she decided to play safe and stay within her dark colour palette.

She opted for a pair of straight blue denim with black shoes, a black crossbody bag, a cream canvas tote (I told you!) and a leopard-printed scarf, which is more like a classic working combination of brown and black dots, rather than yellow and orange screaming print, reminding you of "Animal Planet" straight away.

So, if a stylist recommends you to cheer up your wardrobe with some printed accessories, stop for a minute and inhale some French inspiration first.

Make gentle moves!

In this chapter, I wanted to show you some examples of French ladies taking their outfits to a whole new level by simply adding the right accessories to their classic, plain outfits.

As we all know, brown and grey can make a beautiful colour combination, especially if grey is light and brown is toffee. This is the art of making a statement without going down the slippery road of bright contrasts.

If you have a closer look, you will notice, that the grey coat and grey trousers don't appear boring thanks to their delicate checked print and the same colour socks. The whole silhouette overall doesn't look square or baggy, because the two narrow parts of the body have been cleverly accented: by the belt on the waist and by the length of wide trousers on her ankles.

> 66
> *If I remember correctly, it was a Sunday morning, and this lady was on a relaxing walk with her dog while browsing the shop displays. She was dressed comfortably and smartly, but neither overdone nor too perfect. Good enough to pop into her little favourite café round the corner for a quick cup of espresso if she wanted to.*

Be unique!

Another great
example of
the power of
accessories is the
long navy coat with
black wide cropped
trousers and soft
knitted navy hat,
spiced up by the
red platformed
Converse (an
extremely popular
item in Paris). To
relax the look even
more, she adds a
beige and black
chunky scarf, the
sleeves of her white
sweater and a white
canvas tote (yes,
again!). We can see
that it's another bag
in the picture and
it's also very colour-
coordinated with
the scarf.
**Small, but very
important details.**

To relax the look even more, she adds a beige and black chunky scarf...

Spice it up!

Where are the best spots for "people-watching" in Paris?

Well... It would be corner cafes, but you are risking mistaking tourists for the real locals, because a lot of those cafes are in the middle of the city, and that's exactly where tourists go!

Another place would be Jardin de Tuileries as real Parisians love to spend their time reading a book or enjoying the sun on those cute little chairs around the pond.

But my favourite place to spot authentic French people are these cute local bakeries, tucked away from the main touristy route.

We accidentally bumped into one of those little boulangeries, ordered a couple of coffees and plain croissants and just got lost in the magic of a daily French routine. There was a lady buying three baguettes of a certain type, there was a gorgeous young girl, nervously drinking her hot chocolate while waiting for her date to arrive, there was a couple, debating on the type of croissants they should get. Unforgettable, magical moments, when this French boulangerie just accepted us as a part of its daily routine...

Here we go again... The same long navy coat, which could be possibly belted (if we wanted to), paired with cropped wide leg trousers of some sort of a dark colour, chunky (probably Dr. Martens) boots, a gorgeous raspberry beret and a crossbody bag.

How is the contrast looking so soft? Well... This deep raspberry pink has a lot of blue in it, much more than a classic red, so the whole look appears more harmonious and less pretentious. Also the red beret might look more like a cliché unlike that raspberry pink option.

Part Three
Level Up

Me and my bestie

Dress to impress… yourself!

I like to believe they just met after a long break and are heading for some lunch in a lovely new restaurant just round the corner with a good chance of going somewhere else for a couple of drinks afterwards.

Once again, we have absolutely **iconic colour combinations of beige and black, navy and grey and cream with camel**. As you know by now, colour is not the only thing they pay attention to, it's also the proportions, the shape and the attitude it is worn with.

For example, this gorgeous navy-blue coat definitely looks like a statement piece, at least proportionally. The rest (a grey printed skirt and a grey scarf) is just a complimentary addition to the outfit. Something must always play the main role and the rest will be left to highlight the colour and accent the shape. Even her bag is chosen to be navy, not to break the body in half with a bright contrasting thin strap, unlike the lady on the left, who chose her bag to be a statement.

The strap of her bag is canvas, thick and graphic and it's definitely used to add a fresh contemporary twist to a long classic coat. It's still kept in a mutted colour palette, worn together with the understated chic black trousers and black suede boots.

The third lady is going for the head-to-toe (at least from the back) camel/beige look. She appears much taller because of that and more casual. Her tall suede beige boots definitely elevate the look and her bag (which was in a similar colour palette), adds this effortless and relaxed feeling to her outfit.

Have a good night out ladies! Don't drink too much!

Learning is not copying!

It was a late Saturday morning and I guess it was a mother and daughter who were heading out together to browse through the shops (like French people still do) and kindly showed us a perfect example of styling timeless camel coats in different lengths, shapes and attitudes.

The lady on the left is obviously having a classier approach to styling with this coat. She paired it with dark grey straight full-length trousers, black heeled boots and a black bag. Her coat is belted and perfectly defines her feminine shape, adds the right proportions to the body and elongates her lower half. Have you noticed that soft transition between the graphic grey trousers and black patent boots?

Just imagine for a second that she would opt for a pair of black trousers instead. Unless they are made of a very fluid silky fabric, they would definitely add some formal stiffness to the look.

The lady on the right has lovely wavy caramel hair, complimenting her coat so well. Did I tell you that I've seen an unbelievable number of girls with long hair on the streets of Paris? So, I did. But here you go again as I'm loving it!

Not to appear too classy, this girl adds some loose cream trousers and red sneakers (maybe Converse?) to her outfit, finishing the look with a light trendy-shaped mini-bag in the same colour as her trousers.

Two camel coats, two completely different looks. I would say it's a perfect example of Classic Parisian Style VS New Parisian Classic.

Let your clothes speak for you!

These two ladies were in their late 40s I would say. They were having an interesting modern art related conversation (as far as I could understand). The day was cold and crisp, they were dressed cosily and elegantly. Would you like to have a closer look?

Look at this cream coat on the left: statement, chic, classy and no doubt aristocratic, especially when paired with the wide black trousers and heeled ankle boots.

She could have added some contemporary vibe to the look by pairing her trousers with cream sneakers or an eccentric bright scarf, but obviously, that's not the impression she is after.

Her scarf "coincidentally" consists of big spaced-out squares, resembling the colours of her outfit and I can only imagine how gorgeous her caramel bag is looking on her cream coat from the front.

Her friend went for the whole navy look with a classic knee-length coat, defined with a lovely collar and straight navy jeans, paired with comfy flat camel boots. Her bag is kept in the same colour, in terms of depth and intensity, so it's even hard to tell if it's navy blue or black.

I think we can all agree that those two ladies look extremely good, especially when walking together!

And before I forget, I just wanted to mention that I didn't see a lot of large leather tote bags (so popular all over the world) on the streets of Paris. I would say that women much prefer to have a nice, good-quality small bag for their wallet and keys, paired with a neutral or funky canvas tote for their groceries or other larger items. Well, if you think about it, it makes perfect sense!

Why overload your leather bag with everything you want to put in it and shorten its lifetime if you can invest in a much smaller and better-quality item and keep it in good condition for years to come? All thanks to this canvas tote which is ready to do a heavy-duty job. **Practicality paired with chic – that's the quintessence of Parisian style.**

Care more to care less!

While hunting for my stylish Parisians I made sure none of my strangers was dragging a suitcase or stopping every second to take a picture. Most of them were captured in their daily routine, rushing through the city, having a cigarette, enjoying their shopping or savoring their espresso. My main criterion was attitude... and we need to agree on that, Parisians just have it...

They are marching rather than walking, they are sipping, rather than drinking, they are flirting, rather than talking.

I feel like they are full of contradictions, and they just love it! Black socks with white trousers... no tights with furry coat... wicker basket with leather jacket... High boots with summer dress...Drinking cold wine outside in December and hot espresso in July... Actually no, espresso is an all year-round thing.

On the other hand, these contradictions might help them stay in balance rather than coming down heavily on one or another side. So instead of pairing a classy statement coat with classy boots and classy trousers, they would pair it with lived-in jeans and dirty sneakers.

Is that not a formula for an effortlessly chic look? Oh, and don't forget NOT to brush your hair! Otherwise, you will ruin it all!

These two definitely have this Parisian spirit in them: wavy messy hair, **a long statement coat in the dark colour, some "I couldn't care less" type of jeans, comfy sneakers and a black trusted bag.**

Voila!

**Comfort should be chic,
and chic should be comfortable!**

December 2022. On the way to the Christmas Market. As you can tell, it's slowly getting darker and colder.

Both ladies are ready for a good browse around the stalls, offering spicy Vin Chaud, garlic battered escargots and an endless amount of locally produced craft souvenirs.

The younger girl on the left has a beautiful combination of a dark boxy jacket (probably with quite a few warm layers underneath), paired with cropped light-grey jeans, matching her cosy knitted scarf and chocolate suede boots with soles of a lighter shade. To make the look appear slightly more playful, she adds a crossbody bag in a subtle red colour with a golden chain as a part of her strap.

The lady on the right (as far as we can see) is going for the total noir look, playing on the differences between the textures, where the wide straight fabric of the trousers compliments the satin finish of her puffer jacket and a smooth leather bag in a classic structured shape.

If you think that's all, then you didn't look hard enough…. Yes, she is wearing some red fabric gloves: both warm and chic.

Make your own interpretation!

Classy checked pattern VS Contemporary checked pattern.

I hope you've noticed, that 90 per cent of the outfits we've seen on the streets of Paris so far have one thing in common...

The most popular blank canvas Parisians like to paint on – it's their denim. It could be slim or flared, bleached or raw, short or full length, but there's always a piece of denim involved if we are talking about the effortless Parisian style.

To go with her grey mid-length coat, the lady on the left chooses light-blue, slightly flared denim, paired with white sneakers, which relaxes the overall look and makes it seamless while providing a desirable level of formality.

The younger lady on the right looks more like a rebel. Following the same classic scheme of jeans + coat + scarf, she goes for more unusual shapes, cuts and patterns, which makes the overall look very unique and strong.

However, despite all the modern, boho and Western-inspired ideas, this girl still obeys the well-known classic rules of colour coordination. A light beige checked jacket compliments the colour of her jeans and also reflects some of the colours of this gorgeous scarf (which I believe, thanks to its pattern, goes perfectly with every item in her wardrobe). And don't forget the bag! It's very cool, almost sky-blue (same as some parts of the scarf, and so is the hem on those flared cropped jeans).

This bold statement (as it appears at first) is a highly detailed and still very delicate variation of the classic style with a closer look.

Is it not magical: this moment, which has been captured once, can be seen over and over again and live as long as someone is looking at it!

Couple's Style

Dress tastefully, age gracefully!

Most of the couples you meet in Paris have their own style. And I mean a "couple's style".

Both of them will be elegantly chic or funky playful or bohemian, or effortless, etc. What you will not see is her in fancy high heels and him in a tracksuit.

Why is it happening? Well... If we all agreed that our clothes are a form of self-expression, that means that couples have lots in common. They share their interests, their values, their passion for style, their affection for certain decades in the past or designers in the present day.

A light-mocha jacket on her and a navy trench on him. Both have relaxed bags: his is navy with some cheery stripes, hers is beige and matches her ballet flats. Do they look boring? No, they look chic!

Fun can be chic!

Those two… I remember, they made my day! They were browsing through the pre-loved vintage clothes in the shopping centre Carrousel de Louvre.

They were so cool and enthusiastic, showing each other different pieces, suggesting new outfit ideas. They definitely had their own way of styling hats. They preferred a cosy, roomy, chunky knit, which allows them to play with it.

How do they look ridiculously stylish rather than just ridiculous?

Well… First of all, they had their whole life to practise… Just kidding!

I think the secret is in the right balance of the funky items with classy ones. The most screaming detail of his outfit is those red trousers, but they are supported by the orange shoes, which makes them less eccentric. On top of that, red trousers are absolutely toned down by this taupe jacket, which balances the look and elevates it at the same time.

And our lady dressed in a gorgeous relaxed wine-coloured coat and matching wine trousers. In fact, if she had decided to wear black leather boots instead of her colourful trainers, her look would fall apart.

The bag and hat would look like she borrowed it from her grandkids and it wouldn't work, but supported on three different levels by the matching accessories of similar style, this look appears extremely chic and contemporary at the same time.

Bravo!

Follow your soul call!

I believe that at least one metro station in Paris magically transports people from the 60s and 70s straight to Gare du Nord. I know there could be a more rational explanation: like there are a lot of vintage shops full of authentic clothes around, and lots of young people just craving that aesthetic, but I like my theory better....

Just look at this wide (I believe vinyl) short jacket in an absolutely iconic beige and brown checked print with a defined volume collar. It's kept as a centrepiece of the look and paired with simple caramel (or worn brown) loafers and a crazy canvas tote, splashed with some big graphic flowers in black.

This girl doesn't have thick tights (none of them do in Paris), which makes her legs match the colour of her jacket and elongate the silhouette. Her hair neatly tucked under the collar gives an impression of a nice slick bob.

Her companion has black jeans, trainers, matching with his scarf and a grey bomber. Sounds ordinary, but it does not look boring at all!

What's the secret? First of all, the jeans are straight and cropped, which adds a little bit of innocence and cheekiness to the look; secondly, the trainers are very curvy and sporty in the contrast with his scarf (or at least this dramatic attitude it is worn with). And at last, this bomber not only adds some structure and volume to the look but breaks the dark colour without making too much of a contrast.

I can tell they are a couple. Can you? Do you believe in a couple's style now?

Harmony is the key...

Remember our previous conversation about checked patterns?

Yes, they are not as popular in their usual shape and colours amongst young people, but as always, rather than reaching for completely new patterns, French people just adapt their good old classics. That's how we see a lot of playful checked scarfs on women and lumberjack-style checked jackets on men.

What colour palette can we see here?

It's navy blue for trousers (slightly cheeky navy leopard in her case) and black shoes (with some brown pattern in his).

They both have one bright checked or stripy item which is a centrepiece of their look. It's a shawl for her and a countryside-style cosy jacket for him. Both of those items are light, which elevates the look and contains all the colours of their outfits. Coincidence? No, not this time either...

Oh, and the last note. Her bag... Yes, it's black, but what is so interesting about this bag? What stops it from disappearing into the same colour of her coat? Yes, that's right, this sparkly bit of a golden chain, connected to the leather shoulder strap. Small detail, hardly noticeable, and yet, it's still doing the job.

What colour palette can we see here?

Share your fun a double the joy!

If I asked you to dress classy but not boring, would you go for a bright red backpack and dotted tote?

A lot of us, while thinking about a certain style, imagine directly some items in that style, rather than the way in which things are paired together. But sporty doesn't mean a tracksuit and classy doesn't mean pleated trousers. Style is a way of choosing colours, working with proportions and adding details.

Perhaps this couple can help us a little.

They both have very traditional basic items with an interesting twist, spiced up by some bold statement accessories.

Let's start with this lady wearing a relatively classic checked coat with shortened sleeves and splits on both sides, paired with straight grey trousers and caramel brogues.

It would be a very safe, comfortable and plain combination... But this gorgeous splash of red colour in a beautiful rectangular shape adds to the look strength, youth and edge straight away... She didn't want to be a little bit eccentric; she went full-on. This bright bag covers at least one-third of her body. It's not a detail, it's a statement, toned down by some classy pieces.

Her companion is dressed no less interestingly: grey jeans, a navy blazer and a quirky soft dotted tote in white and navy. Harmonious, chic, modern and classy at the same time!

Split a toffee...

> 66
>
> *I don't think it would be wrong to say that Caramel is one of the most worn colours in Paris (after your staple classics Navy and Black). You can find endless combinations of different shades and intensities of Caramel paired with navy blue (casual), light blue (fresh), off-white (dreamy), brick red (eccentric), silver grey (smart) and finally black (elegant).*

It's common knowledge, that the colours we wear are highly influential on our mood, feelings and self-perception. What if by warming up their wardrobes with soothing Toffee and Camel, French people are replenishing the luck of the sun during the winter season?

How chic and eye-pleasing is this colour combination! How beautiful and subtle this contrast, how balanced and cosy the look is!

A wrap-style caramel coat on her, paired with black leather gloves, skinny black trousers and pointy kitten-heeled ankle boots. She has a medium size brown and beige checked bag to add a little bit of pattern to the look. Still in the same colour palette.

A straight sheepskin caramel jacket on him, paired with grey trousers and black shoes. Simple, tasteful, cosy.

The spirit of Paris

Trends could be expensive, but style is free...

"Wouldn't it be amazing if you could buy your "Je ne sais quoi" on the first floor of Galeries Lafayette amongst the rest of the fancy perfumes and designer sunglasses! No thinking, no trying, no mistakes.

Just go and get it...

But on the other hand, that would mean that only those lucky ones who could afford it would be able to look gorgeous, which is slightly unfair.

The good news is Galeries Lafayette still doesn't sell one, but you can get it despite your budget and the size of your wardrobe.

It's here, it's free, just dare to take it!

Something odd, something new, something borrowed, something blue…

This looks like it's a trusted French formula for that masculine/ feminine look. Blue jeans as a base for a pretty much every outfit, an oversized borrowed jacket, a little trendy detail like a pair of funky sneakers and a ridiculous looking tote.

It was one of those cold winter afternoons, when the sky was already turning dark without even trying to provide any daylight. But in Paris, you don't mind this grey heaven, it goes so nicely together with the colour of sandy buildings and cobbled streets.

You can wrap up warm in your favourite jacket and melancholic thoughts and get lost in your dreams… For a minute, for an hour, for the day. You are in Paris and the city itself tells you to be romantic and sad.

She was a part of Paris… Sitting on the bench on one of the bridges across the Seine looking far away, thinking about something. She seemed sad, but she was present.

A lot of the items in her outfit looked like they belonged to another person (maybe her boyfriend): these straight classic denim jeans, these sporty black and white sneakers, this chunky knit grey hat.

Only her coat still reminded me of a classic Parisian style, but she looked feminine! She still looked feminine! Maybe because of this flock of curls sticking under the hat, maybe her crumpled posture or this massive summery beige canvas tote with funny writing on it.

She was beautiful, she was Parisian…

Live your best life!

He is just rocking it!

I mean… his outfit, his attitude, and probably his day as well!

What a subtle and fresh combination!!

And… Have you noticed?

This look is just saying: yes, I had two minutes before I left the house, so I went for my trusted combination, but I didn't try too hard!

What do you think makes the silhouette so light and cool? Once again, those turned-up trousers, revealing his narrow ankles.

A dark patterned scarf (which I guess has some colours of his outfit in it) and a gorgeous and silly square floral tote, carried in quite an unusual way, which probably adds to the outfit this "a little bit of extra", this unexplainable "Je ne sais quoi".

Create your own palette!

With some of those gorgeous strangers, I was lucky enough to get their looks from a couple of different angles.

This is one of the most interesting outfits to emerge and **one of the best examples to show how knowing your style, your preferences and your colour palette can give you the courage to experiment without looking overdressed.**

This lady uses her hat in a lighter shade of green to support her silky trousers in a darker shade of the same colour. But what is important here is that they are not matching at all! One reminds me of the fresh summer and just watered grass, and the other looks more like some of those gorgeous tasty Italian olives.

The reason, why I'm glad that we have different angles of that look is because from the front you can clearly see that this intriguing colour-block combination of a peachy-cream bag on top of the ocean-blue coat is apparently supported by the beige scarf.

And last but not least: it's a clever way to break the fuss of wearing a hat by adding a pair of colourful trainers to your outfit. Voila!

Take yourself out!

Oh! I remember this one! In fact, I remember them all!

It was our last breakfast in this little Parisian café, tucked away from the main touristy route. The place was full of locals, it was Saturday. Some of them were reading newspapers, some had just arrived to catch up with their friends over a cup of espresso and a fresh baguette. That morning I was mastering the new skill of dipping croissants in my coffee without making a dramatic mess of it.

We arrived quite late so were offered the last but lovely bar-style table near the window looking over this classic Parisian Street. It resulted in a great satisfaction of all our senses at once!

This was an absolute visual indulgence to be able to witness residents of that arrondissement getting on with their morning routine. I managed to capture only one gentleman in dark-burgundy trousers trousers and a chocolate blazer with an effortless scarf wrapped around his neck (I doubt that it was for warmth). His look was so put together and relaxed at the same time, that he didn't appear overdressed at all for a Saturday morning. I think the trick was to wear a close enough top and bottom to look put together rather than going for the total suit and appearing too formal.

But he wasn't the only one! I saw a gorgeous young girl with long wavy hair in a massive bomber and relaxed jeans, and I think in her case it was probably a boyfriend's rather than a "boyfriend style" jacket, and she was rushing back home rather than going to the yoga class. She looked so happy, so young and so in love…

I also saw an elderly lady in a camel coat and an electric blue hat. She looked so cosy, so classy and fresh and once again: it was impossible to guess where she was off to! All those mysterious strangers living their best life.

And why not make it the best?
It's the only life you have!

Why is attention to detail is so important? Because it's a sign of us being present, in tune with a moment, appreciating "now". That's what French culture has mastered...

The skill of being awake and curious, to live in joy starting from something as simple as paying attention to the colour of your socks.

Gradually, you might find yourself looking for some unusual seasoning, which complements the flavour of your favourite chicken dish the most, or choosing another route to go to your work (which takes 10 minutes longer, but the scenery is so much nicer), and overall choosing a better quality of life, day by day...

Simply start by treating everything as an important detail...

I hope you've enjoyed this opportunity to meet my perfect strangers on the streets of Paris.

I hope as well, that you didn't take anything too seriously, as the purpose of this book isn't to state that it's a lucky cast of people who live in Paris and the level of their life is unachievable!

I just noticed that French people definitely know how to enjoy every moment of their daily routine, and how to make an effort even for small occasions like nipping into the nearest boulangerie or taking a dog for a walk.

I wanted to crack their looks to understand their way of thinking, their approach to life, and their self-acceptance.

I hope I wasn't too personal, admiring those looks of my perfect strangers and I hope that this book will become a great source of inspiration for you on a day-to-day basis especially when you need a little bit of a push.

It doesn't take a beret and baguette to look French... Just a little bit of thought before leaving your house and a splash of confidence.

Thank you for walking with me through the streets of Paris one more time!

Au revoir!

Credits, clues and tips

Page 8 Le Babylone is a beautiful café on the way to the Le Bon Marche shopping centre. Cute and fancy.

Page 12 Sugar-crusted choux puffs are my little guilty pleasure and an absolute favourite of the French.

Page 14 Café de Lyon is a classic French corner café with a winter terrace and a beautiful view of the Place de la Bastille.

Page 16 Crème Brule is a dessert you can eat at any time of the day as it is absolutely delicious.

Page 25 Sezane Jumper is an absolute French favourite knitwear brand. Intellectual and comfortable.

Page 33 Comptoir des Cottoniers a modern clothing brand with a classic twist and a masculine touch.

Page 35 Rudolf Stingel temporary photo exhibition in Bourse de Commerce monochromatic and touching.

Page 48 Velvet trousers are an absolute must-have amongst all the French in the winter season.

Page 51 Le velo is a French answer to the gym culture.

Page 53 French pharmacies one of a kind…. A safe haven with qualified staff to solve all your health and beauty issues.

Page 60 Jardin des Tuileries a great place for socialising, sun soaking and relaxing.

Page 85 Leopoldine and the Book of Hours a vibrant painting of a tragically dead Victor Hugo's daughter in his incredibly impressive Maison de Victor Hugo in Paris.

Page 88 Portraits du Grand Siecle du Marais a series of the street displayed portraits of the XVI-century cultural and political influencers of that area.

Page 90 Angelina is a La Belle epoque-inspired tea and fancy pastry house with hot chocolate to die for.

Page 113 Le BHV Marais is a 150-year-old 8-floor temple of trends and style in the heart of Paris.

Page 115 Goutal Paris is a French house of chic perfumes with a little touch of nature and sophistication in one bottle.

Page 125 Marche l'Entrepot a Saint-Ouen is a very special place, where lots of beautifully made pieces from previous centuries restfully wait for their new owners.

Page 126-127 La Smaritane the temple of Parisian luxury, an absolute pearl of the fourth arrondissement, is beautifully arranged in the Art Nouveau style with some Art Deco twist in it.

Page 136 Have you spotted a French lover in the picture? Have a look again... His name is Bobbi...It's one of the most popular models of Jerome Dreyfuss bags among Parisians.

Page 146 Pre-LOVED by CrushON in Carrousel du Louvre abundance of vintage luxury pieces at a fraction of the price.

Page 169 Bourse de Commerce is a place where art lives.

Printed in Great Britain
by Amazon

44666489R00103